THERE ARE MEN
TOO GENTLE
TO LIVE
AMONG WOLVES

JAMES KAVANAUGH

THERE ARE MEN TOO GENTLE TO LIVE AMONG WOLVES

Drawings by Hollis Williford

NASH PUBLISHING   Los Angeles

Library of Congress Catalog Card Number: 75-124414
Standard Book Number: 8402-1141-4

Published simultaneously in the United States and
Canada by NASH PUBLISHING, 9255 Sunset Boulevard,
Los Angeles, California 90069.

Printed in the United States of America

Current printing (last digit):

10 9 8 7 6

OTHER BOOKS BY

James Kavanaugh

A Modern Priest Looks at His Outdated Church

The Birth of God

There Are Men Too Gentle To Live Among Wolves

The Crooked Angel

Will You Be My Friend?

Between Man and Woman

Faces in the City

To

      A cat named Ralph who makes me laugh
        and feel loved
      And a tired old man who makes me cry
        and feel helpless.

But especially to those

      Who can hear the honking of geese
        above the sound of traffic
      Who can hear the weeping of boys
        above the sound of mortars
      Who refuse to take life as it is—
        because it wasn't always.

This is a book born in my heart, born in the pain of ending one life and beginning another, born in the excitement of the continuing search for life's meaning. Some people do not have to search, they find their niche early in life and rest there, seemingly contented and resigned. They do not seem to ask much of life, sometimes they do not seem to take it seriously. At times I envy them, but usually I do not understand them. Seldom do they understand me.

I am one of the searchers. There are, I believe, millions of us. We are not unhappy, but neither are we really content. We continue to explore life, hoping to uncover its ultimate secret. We continue to explore ourselves, hoping to understand. We like to walk along the beach, we are drawn by the ocean, taken by its power, its unceasing motion, its mystery and unspeakable beauty. We like forests and mountains, deserts and hidden rivers, and the lonely cities as well. Our sadness is as much a part of our lives as is our laughter. To share our sadness with one we love is perhaps as great a joy as we can know—unless it be to share our laughter.

We searchers are ambitious only for life itself, for everything beautiful it can provide. Most of all we want to love and be loved. We want to live in a relationship that will not impede our wandering, nor prevent our search, nor lock us in prison walls; that will take us for what little we have to give. We do not want to prove ourselves to another or to compete for love.

This is a book for wanderers, dreamers and lovers, for lonely men and women who dare to ask of life everything good and beautiful. It is for those who are too gentle to live among wolves.

James Kavanaugh
San Diego, 1970

We searchers are ambitious only for life itself, for everything beautiful it can provide. Most of all we want to love and be loved. We want to live in a relationship that will not impede our wandering, nor prevent our search, nor lock us in prison walls; that will take us for what little we have to give. We do not want to prove ourselves to another or to compete for love.

This is a book for wanderers, dreamers and lovers, for lonely men and women who dare to ask of life everything good and beautiful. It is for those who are too gentle to live among wolves.

James Kavanaugh
San Diego, 1970

THERE ARE MEN
TOO GENTLE
TO LIVE
AMONG WOLVES

THERE ARE MEN TOO GENTLE

THERE ARE MEN
TOO GENTLE TO
LIVE AMONG WOLVES

There are men too gentle to live among wolves
Who prey upon them with IBM eyes
And sell their hearts and guts for martinis at noon.
There are men too gentle for a savage world
Who dream instead of snow and children and Halloween
And wonder if the leaves will change their color soon.

There are men too gentle to live among wolves
Who anoint them for burial with greedy claws
And murder them for a merchant's profit and gain.
There are men too gentle for a corporate world
Who dream instead of candied apples and ferris wheels
And pause to hear the distant whistle of a train.

There are men too gentle to live among wolves
Who devour them with eager appetite and search
For other men to prey upon and suck their childhood dry.
There are men too gentle for an accountant's world
Who dream instead of Easter eggs and fragrant grass
And search for beauty in the mystery of the sky.

There are men too gentle to live among wolves
Who toss them like a lost and wounded dove.
Such gentle men are lonely in a merchant's world,
Unless they have a gentle one to love.

LITTLE BOY, I MISS YOU

Little boy, I miss you, with your sudden smile and
      Your ignorance of pain
You walked in life and devoured it—without anything
      But misty goals to keep you company.
Your heart beat mightily when you chased frogs
      And captured one too big for a single hand
You wandered with friends in quiet woods and were
      Startled by a shuffling porcupine
Matches were a mystery that lighted fires and
      Chewed up leaves in savage hunger.
There was no time for meaning—a marshmallow gave it
      On a sharpened stick
A jackknife in your pocket provided comfort when your
      Friends were gone
A flower in the woods hidden by an aging,
      Shriveled log
A dog who danced and licked at your fingers and
      Chewed your jeans
A game of football you didn't expect
      A glass of cider, a cricket's cry.

When did you lose your eyes and ears, when did taste
    Buds cease to tremble;
Whence this sullenness, this mounting fear, this quarrel
    With life—demanding meaning?
The maddening search is leisure's bonus—the
    Pain that forbids you be a boy!

MY EASY GOD IS GONE

I have lost my easy God—the one whose name
    I knew since childhood.
I knew his temper, his sullen outrage, his
    ritual forgiveness.
I knew the strength of his arm, the sound
    of his insistant voice.
His beard bristling, his lips full and red
    with moisture at the moustache,
His eyes clear and piercing, too blue
    to understand all,
His face too unwrinkled to feel my
    child's pain.
He was a good God—so he told me—
    a long suffering and manageable one.
I knelt at his feet and kissed them,
    I felt the smooth countenance of his forgiveness.

I never told him how he frightened me,
    How he followed me as a child
When I played with friends or begged
    for candy on Halloween.
He was a predictable God, I was the
    unpredictable one.
He was unchanging, omnipotent, all-seeing,
    I was volatile and helpless.

He taught me to thank him for the concern
      which gave me no chance to breathe,
For the love which demanded only love in
      return—and obedience.
He made pain sensible and patience possible
      and the future foreseeable.
He, the mysterious, took all mystery away,
      corroded my imagination,
Controlled the stars and would not let
      them speak for themselves.

Now he haunts me seldom: some fierce
      umbilical is broken,
I live with my own fragile hopes and
      sudden rising despair.
Now I do not weep for my sins; I have
      learned to love them
And to know that they are the wounds that
      make love real.
His face illudes me; his voice, with all
      its pity, does not ring in my ear.
His maxims memorized in boyhood do not
      make fruitless and pointless my experience.
I walk alone, but not so terrified as when
      he held my hand.

I do not splash in the blood of his son
　　　nor hear the crunch of nails or thorns
　　　piercing protesting flesh.
I am a boy again—I whose boyhood was
　　　turned to manhood in a brutal myth.
Now wine is only wine with drops that do
　　　not taste of blood.
The bread I eat has too much pride for transubstantiation,
　　　I, too—and together the bread and I embrace,
Each grateful to be what we are, each loving
　　　from our own reality.
Now the bread is warm in my mouth and
　　　I am warm in its mouth as well.

Now my easy God is gone—he knew too
　　　much to be real,
He talked too much to listen, he knew
　　　my words before I spoke.
But I knew his answers as well—computerized
　　　and turned to dogma
His stamp was on my soul, his law locked
　　　cross-like on my heart,
His imperatives tatooed on my breast, his
　　　aloofness canonized in ritual.

Now he is gone—my easy, stuffy God—God,
    the father-master, the mother-whiner, the
Dull, whoring God who offered love bought
    by an infant's fear.
Now the world is mine with all its pain and
    warmth, with its every color and sound;
The setting sun is my priest with the ocean
    for its altar.
The rising sun redeems me with the rolling
    waves warmed in its arms.
A dog barks and I weep to be alive, a
    cat studies me and my joy is boundless.
I lie on the grass and boy-like, search the sky.
    The clouds do not turn to angels, the winds
    do not whisper of heaven or hell.

Perhaps I have no God—what does it matter?
    I have beauty and joy and transcending loneliness,
I have the beginning of love—as beautiful as it
    is feeble—as free as it is human.
I have the mountains that whisper secrets
    held before men could speak,
I have the ocean that belches life on
    the beach and caresses it in the sand,

I have a friend who smiles when he sees
    me, who weeps when he hears my pain,
I have a future full of surprises, a
    present full of wonder.
I have no past—the steps have disappeared
    the wind has blown them away.

I stand in the Heavens and on earth, I
    feel the breeze in my hair.
I can drink to the North Star and shout
    on a bar stool,
I can feel the teeth of a hangover, the
    joy of laziness,
The flush of my own rudeness, the surge of
    my own ineptitude.
And I can know my own gentleness as well,
    my wonder, my nobility.
I sense the call of creation, I feel its
    swelling in my hands.
I can lust and love, eat and drink, sleep
    and rise,
But my easy God is gone—and in his stead
    The mystery of loneliness and love!

TO BEGIN TO LIVE THE REST OF MY LIFE

It makes no sense to my friends back home
That a middle-aged man should want to roam.
But I left the money and a share of fame
And I called it quits in the business game;
I left a house and a proper wife,
    To begin to live the rest of my life.

It makes no sense to my swinging friends
That a middle-aged man should begin again.
So the stories grew and the rumors rolled
As the tale of my madness was oft retold.
But I can bear the gossip's knife
    To begin to live the rest of my life.

It makes no sense to society
That a middle-aged man would take his leave.
The briefcase boys just shook their head,
My mother said I was better off dead.
But I packed my bag without advice
    To begin to live the rest of my life.

It makes no sense to my neighborhood
That a middle-aged man is gone for good.

The preacher bowed his head and prayed,
My father said I should have stayed,
But I went away with the rumors rife
   To begin to live the rest of my life.

Well I'm lonely now but my heart is free,
I enjoy a beer and watch a tree,
I can see a cloud and feel the breeze,
I can buy some bread and a bit of cheese.
And I know full well it is my right
   To begin to live the rest of my life.

Now I have no plans for security,
No proper wife can depend on me,
I'm not too sure of eternity
But I know when a heart is really free.
And I walk along with a step that's light
   To begin to live the rest of my life.

Come with Cain and me
　　　East of Eden towards the sea,
In desert lands called Nod
　　　Where murderers live and lovers
　　　Grown weary of Abel and his God!

WITH
CAIN

The mark upon our face is sadness
And horror is the color of our eyes.
We have seen sights too dark for sunlight,
Known pain unweepable by all the waters of the skies.
We are weary men, too mad for mothers to bear,
Too angry to suck soft breasts of flesh
Lest we bite them to be bathed in blood
And drink the redness, sweet and fresh
For thirst unquenchable in Adam's wells!
We murdered for a father's love—
A trifling price for such a prize.
Now, cast from the garden's dullness,
The honest wastes of Nod are Paradise
For men who took a brother's life to save their own.
He had no life to give, only dullness
And duty with loins as empty as his face
And grinning lips that ate at a father's table,
Where appetite grows too stale to taste

Ought but meat and wine of emptiness
And uttered words that lied like the eyes
That laughed and only seemed to listen,
Too stolid to hear another's cries
Or even weeping!

Come with Cain and me
        East of Eden towards the sea,
In desert lands called Nod

        Where murderers live and lovers
        Grown weary of Abel and his God!

Abel, too weak to kill ought
But the helpless animals in sacrifice,
His body too numb to know ought
But the emptiness of a husbandman's life,
His passion planted like corn and wheat,
His love as lustless as a bleating lamb.
What life had he, this fair and docile man
Of no surprises? Too sweet to damn
A soul to hell, too listless to hate
The silent father whom he served with joy
And comfort and combed his greying hair,
Content to work and whistle like a boy,

Unaware that his blood boiled and spirit burned,
That his heart pulsed with pain
To make love possible.
I am glad the pale wretch is slain,
That once before he died he saw the blood
That dripped from my aching hands
And washed the ground that he tilled
And fed the corn of fertile lands
Where hunger is only nourished and
Bodies are only fed to fall in numbness,
Like the animals made fat to die in dumbness!

Come with Cain and me
     East of Eden towards the sea,
In desert lands called Nod
     Where murderers live and lovers
     Grown weary of Abel and his God!

The lonely are here, they are kind,
Wandering men but they are men
Strong enough to lift the weak and love them,
Silent enough to listen once again
When the lights of paradise beckon
The broken hearts that only wanted a father

To whisper his love if but for a moment,
To look at a child and reverently to gather
Him in arms that all the ages ached for.
The desert days are torrid but the waters are sweet,
And there are palm trees to challenge the sun's cruelness
'Till shadows come at night to thrill the poet
And rest the wanderer in the quiet coolness
Of peace and passion linked in a woman's arms
Strong enough to hold a man's heart,
Gentle enough to touch the sadness on his face,
Wise enough to let him go apart
To dream and wander.

There is silence in the land of Nod
      And peace for lovers brave enough to kill
Come beyond the garden of Abel and his God
      Where men not made for time, lie still!

I DREAM ON WORDS

I dream on words and lick them
    And wonder
How old they are and
    Who created them
When they were only grunts and groans?
Sometimes I'd rather grunt
    Than talk
Because words belong to someone else.
My grunts are my own,
    Lusty in my throat,
    Strong in my chest,
    Born in my belly.
Sometimes I'd rather scream than sing
    Because I write the lyrics
    To my screams.

I dream on words and lick them
    And wonder
Who created them
When they were only sobs and sighs
    Of savages too proud
To go to school
And learn how other men talk.

My sobs are my own,
Caught in my throat,
Heaving in my chest,
Aching in my belly.
Sometimes I'd rather weep than sing
Because I write the music
      For my tears.

Will you come tonight
      And listen
To my symphony
      Of grunts and groans and weeping?

I SAW MY FACE TODAY

I saw my face today
　　　And it looked older,
Without the warmth of wisdom
　　　Or the softness
Born of pain and waiting.
The dreams were gone from my eyes,
　　　Hope lost in hollowness
On my cheeks,
　　　A finger of death
Pulling at my jaws.

　　　So I did my push-ups
And wondered if I'd ever find you,
　　　To see my face
With friendlier eyes than mine.

HEY LIFE!

Hey life!
Is this all you offer
With your circles of sameness
And petty goals giving ulcers to the ambitious,
Your promise of love and meaning and joy,
Your fictitious payoff?

Hey life!
I have seen the somber faces of your children
With a desert's emptiness etched thereon in sadness.
Liquor gives them joy—or a passing romance,
Or a kingdom that offers affluence and fear—
The sun is not enough.

Hey life!
Men drown themselves in conquests and payments,
Women are content to rest submerged in fantasy.
Hatred is as meaningful as hobbies,
Greed gives energy and fear responsibility,
And guilt is fuel enough!

Hey life!
Philosophers stumble and search for meaning,
Studying the heavens to comfort the earth.

There is no comfort—only time to serve,
There is no prison—save that which man makes
And offers to another.

Hey life!
Man is the obedient animal, obedient to you.
He challenges the earth to release its metals
And the heavens to explore its stars.
Only you elude him and mock him
And offer concentric circles.

Hey life!
The pilgrims kept busy, the Christians prayed,
The Jews postponed victory and vengeance like Communists.
Cowards went mad to live as children,
Soldiers hid their pain to win medals,
But most men are vampires.

Hey life!
Men know that you are in the blood
And so they wash themselves in Christ-blood
Or any other kind that makes their cheeks flush
But does not stain their sport coats,
Only their hands.

Hey life!
Man lives never knowing what it means,
Contented by a dash of pleasure and the screams.
His joy—but a moment's respite from pain,
His victory—to know that he is not slain
And can have children!

Hey life!
I see your mocking smile
That hovers over sadness in scorn
Without ever sharing it or even seeing it.
I have no time for you—only for man
Who outlives you!

TO LIVE AMONG WOLVES

FREEDOM

Man does not want freedom,
  He only talks of it,
Satisfied to choose his slavery
  And to pay it homage.

Freedom asks too much:
  Silence and strength,
The death of empty alliances,
  An end to ego baths.

Freedom confronts loneliness
  And lives with it,
Makes more of larks than lust,
  Builds no monuments to itself.

Freedom, content to live without goals,
  Satisfied that living is enough,
Scoffs at titles, laughs at greed,
  Too free to propose reforms.

Man does not want freedom,
  He fears its demands,
And only needs to talk of it—
  The Free Man has no such need.
But man can live without freedom,
  Content to laugh at slavery
And to know today
  That yesterday's pain is gone.

DESPERATE CITY

Desperate city—once young and full of fun!
Dying city—now hidden from the sun!
    The oil is bleeding on your sands,
    The smoke has wrinkled up your hands,
And little children have no place to run.

Desperate city—your heartbeat stilled by noise.
Dying city—no grass for happy boys.
    The traffic drowns your feeble cries,
    The men ignore your tearing eyes,
And trample on the fragments of your toys.

Desperate city—all choked and short of breath.
Dying city—no peace to grant you rest.
    The rebels gather on the street,
    The angry march with heavy feet,
And everywhere the somber talk of death.

Desperate city—deserted by your sons,
Dying city—all shrouded like the nuns!
    The lonely gather in your parks
    And wait in vain to hear the larks
And in the distance sound the roaring guns.

Desperate city—sadder than you seem.
Dying city—without a saving dream.
    I hear the rasping in your chest,
    And see the wounds upon your flesh
And wait to hear your last protesting scream!

    Desperate city—I have loved you so!
Dying city—I'll bury you in snow!

HOW CAN YOU LIVE IN KANSAS

How can you live in Kansas
    And expect anything to change?
How can you seek new answers
    When you ride the endless plain?
I'd sit astride my pinto nag
    To survey my sprawling acres,
My back would slope, my knees would sag,
    I'd have no truck with "fakers."
I'd breathe fresh air and boldly dare
    To rule my sprawling range,
How can you live in Kansas
    And expect anything to change?

LITTLE WORLD

Little world, full of little people shouting for
    recognition, screaming for love,
Rolling world, teeming with millions, carousel of
    the hungry,
Is there food enough? Wheat and corn will not do.
The fat are the hungriest of all, the skinny the most
    silent.
Little, rolling world, you smother me and make me lonely,
Only a few can mount you; the rest must ride on other men
And suck out all their blood even as they whisper of love.
Little world without answers, rolling steadily on your
    empty axis,
Tempting each helpless man to conquer and bind you,
Knowing that when he possesses you—all neatly trussed—
    he does not have enough
But searches out other worlds or yearns for life and blood.
The cannibals were more honest, little world, they
    sucked flesh sincerely
And cooked it tenderly—not tearing it from the bone,
Nor heaping it upon the floor. They ate it.

Little world, mocking schemes of reconstruction,
Battleground of demogogues, burial ground of lonely
    men made dizzy by your stubbornness,

You bury miners in your bowels—you bury free men as well
And sift their ashes in the smog-filled wind.
You are the most heartless of all worlds because you
       feel no pain,
Laughing at the dreamers who struggle to give you life,
Lashing at the poets who offer you a planet's course.
Strange! Little world, I never knew you as a planet
Rolling free in the heavens and strutting for the yellow moon.
Men weigh you down, rising cities make you too heavy to roll.
You are motionless to me—cats make more sense.
You never lick my hand nor show your wounds,
You sadden me with all your rage and blood—you frighten me!

Little world, full of scars and gashes, ripened with another's
       pain,
Your flowers feed on carrion—so do your birds;
Men feed on each other because you taught them life was cheap,
Flowing from your endless womb without pain or understanding.
No midwife caresses your flesh or bathes clean your progeny,
Life spurts from you, little world, and you regard it with
       disdain.
Only bruised men sense your cruelty, men whose life has
       lost its meaning.
You drip with blood, little world, and the Arctic's coldness,

You sweat with tropic heat and bury bitter memories in
    your desert sands.
Whence your pride, little world? Men gave your minerals meaning,
Struggling men gave value to your land when they sold it
    for a profit.
You knew not you were a planet till brave and greedy men
    told you,
And yet you trample on the messengers that pay you homage
And offer them no more than the blind beggar that sits in
    your dusty lap.

Little world, I will not fight for your approval,
I will not fear your sullenness and scorn,
I will enjoy your waves and gentle valleys. You cannot enjoy—
You roll around and mock men as fools,
But they are worth all of you, little world, and more.
A sparrow knows pain, you only know the arrogance of your
    rolling ride.
Somehow man will outlive you, somehow so will I.
Your rolling will cease, so will the wind of your mocking
    laugh.
Other planets will roll in your place when your motor is
    run down,
But man will endure because he is not afraid to weep

And to reach for another's hand when your towering trees
     have scourged him
And left him limp and bleeding in the sullen darkness of
     your forests,
Or when your waves, answering the lust of the moon,
Have spit him up upon the coldness of your sands.
You will only roll and mock the infants who make your grass
     green,
Who nourish your trees and climb mountains to look beyond you.
The poet sits astride you, little world, dizzy with your
     mad motion, but unafraid.
Your depths boil, your rock heart breaks, your surface
     crumbles,
And your stored-up rage spews upon the innocent.
Blood flows in your jungles and mingles with your
     tearless rivers.
But man will search for love and hope long after you have
     ceased to roll.
Even now he orbits other planets in his distrust of you,
Searching for a better world, one that rolls not in mockery,
And each blast-off promises him life—even as it toasts
     your everlasting death!

COME TO THE BEACH WITH ME

Come to the beach with me
  And watch the pelicans die,
Hear their feeble screams
  Calling to an empty sky
Where once they played
  And scouted for food,
Not scavenging like the gulls
  But plummeting unafraid
Into friendly waters.

Come to the beach with me
  And watch the pelicans die,
Listen to their feeble screams
  Calling to an empty sky.
Maybe Christ will walk by
  And save them in their final toil
Or work a miracle from the shore,
  A courtesy of Union Oil.

Come to the beach with me
  And watch the pelicans die.
My God! They'll never fly again.
  It's worse than Normandy somehow,
For there we only murdered men.

I PLAYED GOD TODAY

I played God today
   And it was fun!
I made animals that men had never seen
So they would stop and scratch their heads
   Instead of scowling.
I made words that men had never heard
So they would stop and stare at me
   Instead of running.
And I made love that laughed
So men would giggle like children
   Instead of sighing.
Tomorrow, perhaps, I won't be God
And you will know it
   Because you won't see any three-headed cats
   Or bushes with bells on . . .
I wish I could always play God
   So lonely men could laugh!

THE BLACKS
ALL MARCH

The blacks all march to invade the sanctuaries where
   Fat men eat themselves to death
     To silence their wives,
   And garrulous women fill their lonely stomachs
     To silence their wombs.
   Calories replace fondling when hands are too heavy
     To hold ought but forks and knives.

   Spaghetti can be sensuous, you know,
     And easy on the lips.
   "Come to me, my cherrystone clam,
     And lose your hymen!
   Warm to me, my garlic scampi,
     I leave big tips
   For headwaiters who smile for silver
     And bow with dash,
   Like mistresses who seduce the desperate ones for cash."

The blacks all march to invade the sanctuaries where
   Sex seems senseless or has petered out
     Before escargots,
   And ladies talk of astrology and saints
     Who died from fasting,

Virgo's and Leo's and saintly padre Pio's
  —Delicate bons mots—
With steaks delicately done to seal off vaginas
  Grown medium rare,
And chops that fall from the bone
  Like middle-aged lust.
The soufflé flops like sagging breasts
  Too tired to bare
Dry nipples framed like cheese on melba toast,
  With crispy crust
And wastelines that double the square of the bust.

The blacks all march to invade the sanctuaries where
  Weary wallets ask American Express
    To pay the bill
And headwaiters fuss a bit to enhance the kill
    Of fat men too tired to rape ought but sirloins,
Who later hide their billfolds in dresser drawers
    When aching loins
Plead for a prostitute to strip
  For the price of a meal,
And dodging rolls of meat
  Emits a squeal

More pleasing than the cynical smile of a waiter,
More joyous than the dull thud of a wife. He can't hate her
   So he takes her to dinner all preened in her Saks
Away from the marching of the desperate blacks.

The blacks all march to invade the sanctuaries where
   Fat men feed their wives and silently stare.

OLD MAN

Old man—what has life done to you?
God! For you, old man, I would create a heaven,
So merciless has life been on the earth.
Your eyes so pure and blue,
Childlike now and hollow in their sockets,
Your body feeble and almost spent,
Only the spirit that still beats in it,
Reminds me that it is yours.
Antiseptic hands care for you and prod you when
        you quarrel like the child you could never be.
Damn the life that took me from you!
Damn the world that keeps you alive
And shoves you aside.
Damn me for forgetting you in the agony of present pain.
I love you, old man, feeble old man
With rumpled hat,
Fighting old man who will struggle
        Fiercely 'till the day he dies.
Not paranoia this, as learned doctors diagnose—
Only a tired old man who has lost the sophisticated
        pretense that obscured
        your lonely struggle and locked it wordlessly
        in your heart!

WELCOME TO OAKWOOD GARDENS APARTMENT COMPLEX

Welcome to Oakwood Gardens Apartment Complex
    Where society rewards its heroes
With health salons and sauna baths
    And pool tables and karate lessons
Or bridge and investment counselling
    And Sunday morning coffee by the pool
With Hawaiian punch if you come early
    —Courtesy of Mr. Oakwood, I presume—
Who designed his antiseptic Gardens
    Free from cats and dogs and children
To keep pollution down and preserve the grey rugs
    Where soft butts can sit without bruises
To talk of saving the world from smog and overpopulation
    And dire things like poverty among the poor
Who forget to take the pills designed by the chemists
    Clean enough to swim in Mr. Oakwood's pool without showering.

Welcome to Oakwood Gardens Apartment Complex
    Where life is not complex at all
And an aging Beatrice introduces the circles of survival
    To customers who finally deserve to enjoy life
And additional sun in the morning for ten dollars more a month,
    —Courtesy of Mr. Oakwood, I presume—

And cable television free of charge
  To catch the latest movies from L.A.
And trees properly spaced to remind you of other times
  When the land was lavish with its trees—and even careless
With its flowers.

Welcome to Oakwood Gardens Apartment Complex
  Where Miami Hotels are available to everyone
Who arrives early enough for a beach chair
  Which gives you a place by the pool
Where Mecca comes to Muhammad with the sun properly angled
  For the most salutary effects available to a nuclear man
Who left his clan in rural Pennsylvania to earn his freedom
  —Courtesy of Mr. Oakwood, I presume—
And to find friends who express their independence
  By the pictures they hang on the walls
Without marring the plaster which Mr. O. so thoughtfully provided,
  And I mustn't forget the grey rugs which are soft to sit on.

So welcome to Oakwood Gardens Apartment Complex
  With immediate occupancy for the lonely who are looking for love
And better barbeques than they had anywhere else

With tennis lessons and scuba diving thrown in free,
—Courtesy of Mr. Oakwood, I presume—
And music piped into the recreation center
Where the clubs can meet without extra dues,
And soon we will have our own church
To thank the God of Oakwood Gardens Apartment Complex
Who is, I presume, the courtesy of Mr. Oakwood.

THE FOOTBALL GAME

The gods assemble on the gridiron
To sanctify Sunday for the lonely
Who bury their fears in the cheers for their heroes
And munch hot dogs in ritual communion.
The giants on the earth are gathered on Sunday
Like priests with upraised arms
To silence the heavens
And bleeding bodies bruised in sacrifice
To atone for loneliness
Of faces grown pale and bloodless in desperation
And a world's silence!

The gods assemble on the gridiron
To sanctify Sunday in padded vestments
And shout their psalmic signals to the sun,
While marching bands make music
Stomping on the bloody sand
And chorus girls give hope to tired men
Whose loins are too timid for battle
Save the vicarious kind
Where padded Christs imprison life
In a violent cross buck,
And nail hands and feet that dare to stray
In stubborn confrontation.

The gods assemble on the gridiron
To sanctify Sunday and thus to brighten Monday
When life must be lived again and the mounting pain
Erodes the colors of victory and the freedom
Of a sudden touchdown.
The little men who taste life's ashes
Can spit them out long enough to cheer for giants
Who walk above the earth, tall enough to see the sky,
To challenge trees, to move the grey buildings from
Their dull foundation.

The gods assemble on the gridiron
To sanctify Sunday for men too timid to fight
Their wives or hated jobs or even the dullness
Of themselves.
Who choose instead to make another's dreams
A sign of victory and wring their hands
In mythic union with the bleeding, bruising
Ritual below.
Where Eagles and Falcons feed on carrion to conquer
Vikings and Chargers from a distant world,
Where Lions and Rams with fierce appetites
Chew the Redskins in their Warrior's paints
And make a banquet on the bodies of Saints!

The gods assemble on the gridiron
To sanctify Sunday for men grown weary of church
And hymns and sacraments too subtle
For the viciousness of life
And services too gentle for men who feel the
Teethmarks of time and the wounds of
Mounting despair.
The giants on the earth are gathered on Sunday
In huddles held to promise victory
Over arms and legs that claw and smother, hands
That lust for murder and feet that kill—
A proper ritual for the wandering, lonely men
Who have lost their will.

The gods are gathered on the gridiron
Without mercy or reprieve,
And lonely men assemble in the distance
Afraid to live—or leave!

LONELY NUMBERED CARDS

Beyond the churches where men stand tall enough to talk to God,
Beyond the cities where men are kind enough to pause and nod,
Along the highways that lead to everywhere and none,
There is a bar where lonely men and women come.
Where music, alcohol, and swaying bodies all conspire
To deaden pain, to heal unwhispered wounds with fire
Of flesh aroused from sleep and then to meet again
Some other night, some other lonely place when
Men and women shuffled in loneliness meet by chance
Like queens and kings to weep and share a dance
Beyond the churches, beyond the fenced-in yards,
Where there are no people, but only numbered cards.

And on the night I was the loneliest of all,
I won you in a final midnight draw
And fondled you not listening to your name
Or caring save to play the lonely game,
To heal a wound grown deep and hard
And feel the warmth of another numbered card,
Until I saw your eyes so sad and vast
With dreams of home and children splattered in your past
And touched your hand to feel the stain of tears
To share with you the pain of secret fears!

And for an instant you and I were real
Despite the fantasy of place and fated deal
Before we wandered off again to tangled dreams
To bear in loneliness the hurt of silent screams
Beyond the churches and the fenced-in yards
Where there are no people but lonely numbered cards.

THE CITY

At night the city's like a forest,
    The cars like fireflies
And all the buildings reaching up,
    Like trees support the skies.

The people move like little bugs
    And run from tree to tree,
Only differing in their size
    And colored finery.

At night the city's like a forest
    The cars like fireflies,
And all the buildings reaching up
    Like trees support the skies.

And desperately in loneliness
    I run from tree to tree,
And hope that in my wandering
    Some bug will fancy me!

MARIA

Maria, lonely prostitute on a street of pain,
You, at least, hail me and speak to me
While a thousand others ignore my face.
You offer me an hour of love,
And your fees are not as costly as most.
You are the madonna of the lonely,
The first-born daughter in a world of pain.
You do not turn fat men aside,
Or trample on the stuttering, shy ones,
You are the meadow where desperate men
Can find a moment's comfort.

Men have paid more to their wives
To know a bit of peace
And could not walk away without the guilt
That masquerades as love.
You do not bind them, lovely Maria, you comfort them
And bid them return.
Your body is more Christian than the Bishop's
Whose gloved hand cannot feel the dropping of my blood.
Your passion is as genuine as most,
Your caring as real!

But you, Maria, sacred whore on the endless pavements of pain,

You, whose virginity each man may make his own
Without paying ought but your fee,
You who know nothing of virgin births and immaculate conceptions,
You who touch man's flesh and caress a stranger,
Who warm his bed to bring his aching skin alive,
You make more sense than stock markets and football games
Where sad men beg for virility.
You offer yourself for a fee—and who offers himself
For less?

At times you are cruel and demanding—harsh and insensitive,
At times you are shrewd and deceptive—grasping and hollow.
The wonder is that at times you are gentle and concerned,
Warm and loving.
You deserve more respect than nuns who hide their sex
For eternal love;
Your fees are not so high, nor your prejudice so virtuous.
You deserve more laurels than the self-pitying mother
Of many children,
And your fee is not as costly as most.

Man comes to you when his bed is filled with brass
And emptiness,

When liquor has dulled his senses enough
To know his need of you.
He will come in fantasy and despair, Maria,
And leave without apologies.
He will come in loneliness—and perhaps
Leave in loneliness as well.
But you give him more than soldiers who win medals and pensions,
More than priests who offer absolution
And sweet-smelling ritual,
More than friends who anticipate his death
Or challenge his life,
And your fee is not as costly as most.

You admit that your love is for a fee,
Few women can be as honest.
There are monuments to statesmen who gave nothing to anyone
Except their hungry ego,
Monuments to mothers who turned their children
Into starving, anxious bodies,
Monuments to Lady Liberty who makes poor men prisoners.
I would erect a monument for you—who give more than most—
And for a meager fee.

Among the lonely, you are perhaps the loneliest of all,

You come so close to love
But it eludes you
While proper women march to church and fantasize
In the silence of their rooms,
While lonely women take their husbands' arms
To hold them on life's surface,
While chattering women fill their closets with clothes and
Their lips with lies,
You offer love for a fee—which is not as costly as most—
And remain a lonely prostitute on a street of pain.

You are not immoral, little Maria, only tired and afraid,
But you are not as hollow as the police who pursue you,
The politicians who jail you, the pharisees who scorn you.
You give what you promise—take your paltry fee—and
Wander on the endless, aching pavements of pain.
You know more of universal love than the nations who thrive on war,
More than the churches whose dogmas are private vendettas
Made sacred,
More than the tall buildings and sprawling factories
Where men wear chains.
You are a lonely prostitute who speaks to me as I pass,
And I smile at you because I am a lonely man.

A GENTLE ONE TO LOVE

WHERE ARE
YOU HIDING
MY LOVE?

Where are you hiding my love?
  I have sought you so long
That surely you must feel the pulsing
  Of my endless longing!
The words I speak in the night's silence
  And in the fears of early morning.
Each day I know you must be waiting
  For my hand to lead you
From some novitiate
  Where the wind has softened your hands
And the rain has washed your waiting eyes.

Where are you hiding my love?
  I have sought you since childhood
When the first rustle of a woman's skirt
  And the gentleness of her voice
Filled me with some fierce appetite
  For wordless wisdom in the silence of your arms.
I was looking in the subways and the stores
  And in the endless motion of the streets,
In proper parties and in the lonely booths
  Of dark and quiet bars.

I care not whose you were—or even whose you are—
    Your eyes will tell me that you are mine
And that you are waiting.

Where are you hiding my love?
    Till now my life has been a fool's mission
And wise men mock the madness of my searching.
    My work is but ashes, my talents only unshed tears
That flow like rivers in my desperate thirst for you.
    So long I have crushed the panting maidens
Who did not know my passion only writhed
    In lonely longing for your embrace.
My boiling blood that roused my manhood
    To some fleshy sword of searching
Only sought you and spent itself a thousand times
    In sadness and wilting disappointments
In another's barren bed.

Where are you hiding my love?
    Even now the days and nights alone
Have clawed at your heart and marked your face
    With the frowns of loneliness flanking your lips.

Your throat is choked as it longs to sound my name,
    Your breasts are heavy as they wait to feel the pressure
Of my own aching chest,
    Your womb is anxious as it waits to feel my life.
O God! I have sought you for centuries,
    Accepted weak symbols of your promise,
Torn at gates that only led to darkness
    And increased appetite for you,
Swore I would not live another day without your love.

Where are you hiding my love?
    Each day without you will never come again.
Even today you missed a sunset on the ocean,
    A silver shadow on yellow rocks I saved for you,
A squirrel that ran across the road, a duck diving for dinner.
My God! There may be nothing left to show you
Save wounds and weariness and hopes grown dead,
    And wilted flowers I picked for you a lifetime ago,
Or feeble steps that cannot run to hold you,
    Arms too tired to offer you to a roaring wind,
A face too wrinkled to feel the ocean's spray.

Where are you hiding my love?
    Please come to me at twilight when the light
Is as soft as your breasts and the cool air
    Will turn your longing breath into misty drops of love,
When soon enough the darkness will be upon us,
    The quiet time when words have lost their meaning
And only eyes can speak or lips that explore
    Without a sound or syllable to impede their tasting.
Please stay, my love, and share the life I saved for you,
    Each drop of it guarded against all invasion till now.

Where are you hiding my love?
    I wait in hope and sorrow.
Where are you hiding my love?
    Will you come? Tomorrow?

ONLY I WILL KNOW

Come tell me of your sadness
Where the forest flowers grow
   Where the whispering breeze
   Binds the lips of the trees
And only I will know!

Come tell me of your secret fears,
Where the beach is soft as snow
   Where the sparkling spray
   Binds the eyes of the day
And only I will know.

Come tell me of your special dreams
Where the roaring rivers flow
   Where the white water blocks
   All the ears of the rocks
And only I will know.

Come tell me of your deepest joys
Where the desert winds still blow
   Where the shifting of sand
   Hides the face of the land
And only I will know.

Come tell me of your fondest hopes
Where the mountains look below
    Where a gathering cloud
    Cloaks the peaks in its shroud
And only I will know.

Come tell me all, my darling,
As we saunter in the snow
    Where the chill of the night
    Robs the goblins of sight
And only I will know.

Come tell me all, my darling,
When the land is wet with rain
    When the tears blind the eyes
    Of the curious skies
And only I will know!

SOFT AND SILENT

Everything I love is soft and silent,
  My cat, the morning, the end of day,
Even the moon in its way.

Everything I love is soft and silent,
  The water, the forest, the snow at play,
Even the mountain in its way.

Everything I love is soft and silent,
  The sun on the sand, a rainy day,
Even the wind in its way.

Everything I love is soft and silent,
  The grass, the brook, the leaves at play,
Even you in your way.

THAT'S THE WAY

"Do not talk so much," said he.
"That's the way that women are," said she,
"So love me!"

"Do not spend so much," said he.
"That's the way that women are," said she,
"So love me!"

"Do not mother me," said he.
"That's the way that women are," said she,
"So love me!"

Then one day, he went away,
Sorry that he couldn't stay.
"How can you treat me thus?" asked she.
"That's the way I am," said he,
"So love me!"

MAYBE IF YOU'D KNOWN ME AS A CHILD

Maybe if you'd known me as a child
    When I shovelled snow
And told the lady
    That a dollar was too much
For a medium sidewalk
    Without ice,
You would have loved me.
    Or when I bought a sugar bowl
For my mother's birthday
    And had it gift wrapped
With the price inside.

Maybe if you'd known me as a child
    And seen me laughing on the grass
When Georgie tickled me
    And poured his Pepsi
On my belly button
    You would have loved me.
Or when I ransomed pagan babies
    For the nuns
For a dollar each

    And gave them names
Like Adam to the animals.

Maybe if you'd known me as a child,
    Then when we sat together
The night I left
    Not knowing what to say
After all the times of trying
    You would have loved me!

REMEMBER WHEN WE LAUGHED

Remember when we sat in silence
    To watch a nibbling fawn come near?
Remember when we saw the fishermen
    Unload their slippery sea bass on the pier?
. . . Remember when we laughed?

Remember when we slept in forests
    —I kissed the morning's mist upon your face?
Remember when we swam at midnight
    And warmed our naked bodies in embrace?
. . . Remember when we laughed?

Remember when we walked to rivers
    And hungrily made love upon the ground?
Remember when we ate with candles
    To gaze in special words we couldn't sound?
. . . Remember when we laughed?

Remember when our hearts were empty,
    When words were only scabs to hide our blood?
Remember when our eyes grew stony
    When rain upon the ground was only mud?
. . . Remember when we laughed?

REMEMBER DARLING

Remember, darling, when you wandered in my loneliness
    And climbed the hills you never climbed before.
You walked all bruised and bloody on the sharp stones
    within me,
And with the blood you caressed my aching flesh.
Dark caves opened to you, pools of tears where only I
    had been before.
Quiet and raging caverns of love heretofore unexplored.

And you took me into the ghettoes of your own fears,
    and said words you could not say before—even
    as your fingers dug my flesh.
Pretense disappeared and the tinseled lustre of artifice
    dissolved.
My God, we were real—arms and legs entwined, naked
    and unashamed.
And when I rose up and tore at your body's door, I
    glided within,
And felt your very spirit merge with mine.
And all the passion of the past was as nothing—
    those greedy, searching hands that knew not what
    they sought,

The gasping, grasping lust for life only a symbol of
        the reality that now we knew.
I had never kissed before, never known the washing of
        your lips,
And as our bodies rose to ecstasy, our spirits joined
        the chorus of our flesh.
We swam together in a rolling ocean of life and love.
And in an instant I knew my need to live near water
        and to hear its voice,
To sense its drive, its rage, its peace and power,
To know the suddenness of storms upon the lake, the foam
        of the ocean, the sparkle of the salty waves, the
        ripple of the running brook.
It was the love I longed for in my loneliness—the
        love the water promised and described.

And in your arms—our flesh mingling with the salt of
        sweat and tears—I was the ocean and so were you,
And so was all of life: rolling and sighing, moaning
        and pleading for love.
Then quietly we lay—never strangers again—never
        hiding so desperately the darkness of our souls.

We had opened to love—perhaps but a glimpse of it—and
as I tasted your flesh, for the first time I tasted
the sweetness of my own.
And amid the chaos of the waters, the rolling of its waves,
a spirit hovered, our spirit . . .
And in the midst of the water there was land to cling to—
it was our creation and it was good.

THE QUIET MORNINGS

I like the quiet mornings
When the waves have washed the footprints from the shore,
When even the gulls are just beginning to stir
And the heat of the day has not yet aroused the flies to search
    the seaweed for breakfast,
When the beach still has the sand of sleep in its eyes
And the driftwood looks like tired swimmers resting on the shore,
When the waves laugh at the rocks
And playfully wash the night from their eyes.

Soon enough the hungry gulls will dive for fish
And the waves will beat shape into the rocks.
Feet will pound on the beach
And ladies will snatch the driftwood for lamps,
And I will face the day's demands,
Trampled like the sand,
Wounded like the rocks,
Torn up like the wood,
Living for another quiet morning!

IN THE CENTER OF YOUR SOUL

There is quiet water
    In the center of your soul,
Where a son or daughter
    Can be taught what no man knows.

There's a fragrant garden
    In the center of your soul,
Where the weak can harden
    And a narrow mind can grow.

There's a rolling river
    In the center of your soul,
An eternal giver
    With a rich and endless flow.

There's a land of muses
    In the center of your soul,
Where the rich are losers
    And the poor are free to go.

So remain with me, then,
    To pursue another goal
And to find your freedom
    In the center of your soul.

ABOUT THE AUTHOR

James Kavanaugh, poet and philosopher, is the well-known former priest who wrote the revolutionary books *A Modern Priest Looks at His Outdated Church* and *The Birth of God*. As a clinical psychologist, he coauthored the remarkable study of human relationships called *Between Man and Woman*. He has also written a touching children's story called *The Crooked Angel*.

In the last few years he has been recognized by growing numbers of people as an outstanding contemporary poet—unpretentious, uniquely aware, explosive, in touch with the full range of human feelings. *There Are Men Too Gentle To Live Among Wolves* is his first book of poetry; it was followed by *Will You Be My Friend?* (1971) and most recently by *Faces in the City*. *There Are Men Too Gentle To Live Among Wolves* is also available on LP record with the author reading selections from his own book.

James Kavanaugh lives on the top floor of an 80-year-old Victorian house in San Francisco.

```
        #802  08-17-2007 4:53PM
     Item(s) checked out to patron

TITLE: There are men too gentle to live
BC: 3 2091 00015 9203
DUE: 09-07-07


SAINT PAUL PUBLIC LIBRARY - RENEW ITEMS:
   651-292-6002 or www.sppl.org/renew
```